Score

FLE✗IBLE PRAISE

Selected by James Curnow

CURNOW®
MUSIC

FLEXIBLE PRAISE

is the second edition in the Curnow Music Press flexible ensemble series and has been designed with the sacred ensemble conductor in mind. Arranged by internationally know composers/arrangers, these ten pieces will work well with every instrumental ensemble imaginable, including quartets of mixed instruments, praise bands, full band or orchestra, and brass band. The arrangements are designed to be playable by an average grade 3 (strong middle school or average high school) player. Each arrangement includes optional descant (fifth part), keyboard (with chords included for use with guitar), percussion (mostly drum set) and electric bass parts. These parts enhance the overall sound of the arrangement, but are not required for performance. This gives the conductor unlimited ways to use the arrangements.

My prayer, and the prayer of the arrangers, is that you will be able to use any or all of these pieces in whatever type of worship and praise service you may be called upon to participate.

In Christ,

James Curnow

President

Curnow Music Press

Order Number: CMP 1234-08-401

James Curnow
FLEXIBLE PRAISE
Conductor

ISBN 978-90-431-2940-4

HOW TO USE FLEXIBLE PRAISE

As long as there is one player on each of the four main parts, these arrangements will work. In fact, if you have only one or two instrumentalists and play Part 1 and 2, along with the piano (and possibly bass and drums), these arrangements will still be extremely effective. After each of those four parts is covered, it is up to the conductor to decide how the other instruments will be used (see chart below for instrumentation possibilities). The possibilities are unlimited. Once instrumentation is established, the conductor of larger ensembles can choose to have just woodwinds, brass or strings play specific sections in order to provide variety in timbre. Another possibility would be to select any of the four main parts to be played by just woodwinds, brass, or strings.

Available books

PART NAME	INSTRUMENTATION	ORDER NUMBER
Descant C	Flute, Oboe, Bells, Violin	CMP 1235-08-401
Descant B♭	B♭ Clarinet, B♭ Trumpet	CMP 1236-08-401
Part 1 C	Flute, Oboe, Bells, Violin	CMP 1237-08-401
Part 1 B♭	B♭ Clarinet, B♭ Trumpet	CMP 1238-08-401
Part 1 E♭	E♭ Alto Saxophone, E♭ Trumpet, E♭ Clarinet	CMP 1239-08-401
Part 2 C	Violin	CMP 1240-08-401
Part 2 B♭	B♭ Clarinet, B♭ Trumpet	CMP 1241-08-401
Part 2 F	F Horn, English Horn	CMP 1242-08-401
Part 2 E♭	E♭ Alto Saxophone, E♭ Alto Horn	CMP 1243-08-401
Part 3 B.C.	Bassoon, Trombone, Euphonium, Cello	CMP 1244-08-401
Part 3 B♭	B♭ Tenor Saxophone, B♭ Euphonium T.C.	CMP 1245-08-401
Part 3 F	F Horn	CMP 1246-08-401
Part 3 E♭	E♭ Alto Clarinet, E♭ Alto Saxophone, E♭ Alto Horn	CMP 1247-08-401
Part 3 C	Viola	CMP 1248-08-401
Part 4 B.C.	Bassoon, Trombone, Euphonium, Tuba, Cello, Double Bass	CMP 1249-08-401
Part 4 B♭ T.C.	B♭ Bass Clarinet, B♭ Contra Bass Clarinet, B♭ Euphonium T.C., B♭ Bass T.C.	CMP 1250-08-401
Part 4 E♭ T.C.	E♭ Contralto Clarinet, E♭ Baritone Saxophone, E♭ Bass T.C.	CMP 1251-08-401
Keyboard	Piano, Synthesizer, Organ (Guitar Chords included)	CMP 1252-08-401
Percussion	Drum Set	CMP 1253-08-401
Electric Bass	Electric Bass, Double Bass	CMP 1254-08-401
Score		CMP 1234-08-401

TABLE OF CONTENTS

JUST A CLOSER WALK

Arr. James Curnow (ASCAP)

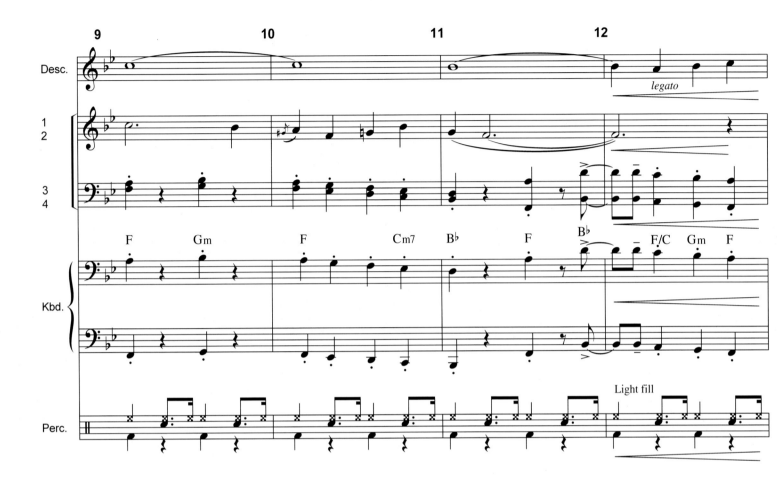

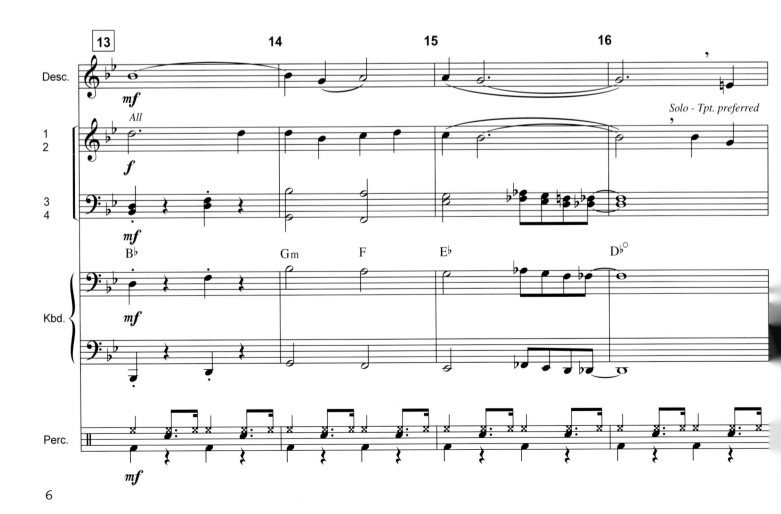

8

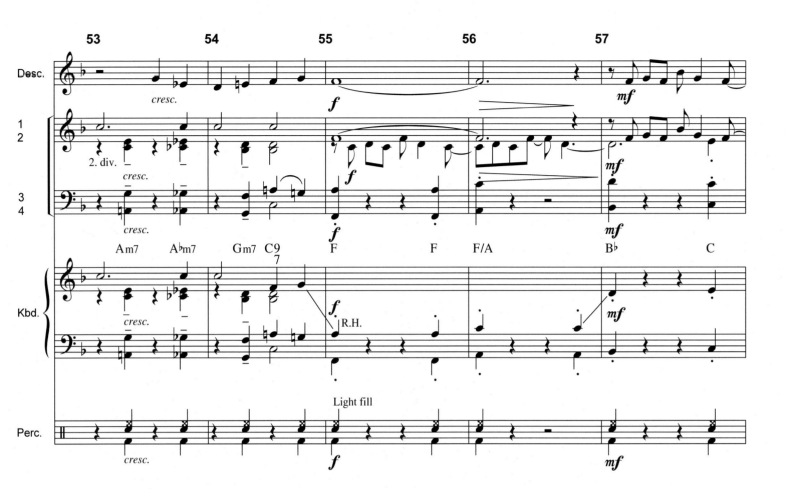

LET US ADORE HIM

Worship Medley

Timothy Johnson (ASCAP)

ON TO VICTORY!

Onward, Christian Soldiers

Arthur Sullivan
Arr. James Curnow (ASCAP)

RELIANCE

How Firm a Foundation

Paul Curnow (ASCAP)

24

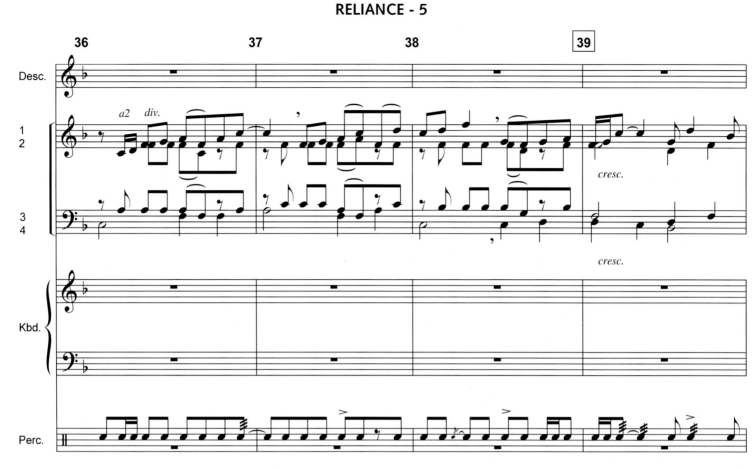

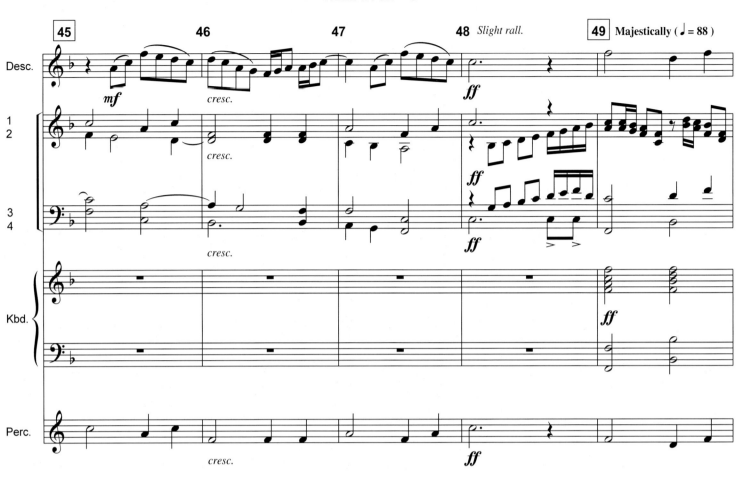

REJOICE THE LORD IS KING

Douglas Court (ASCAP)

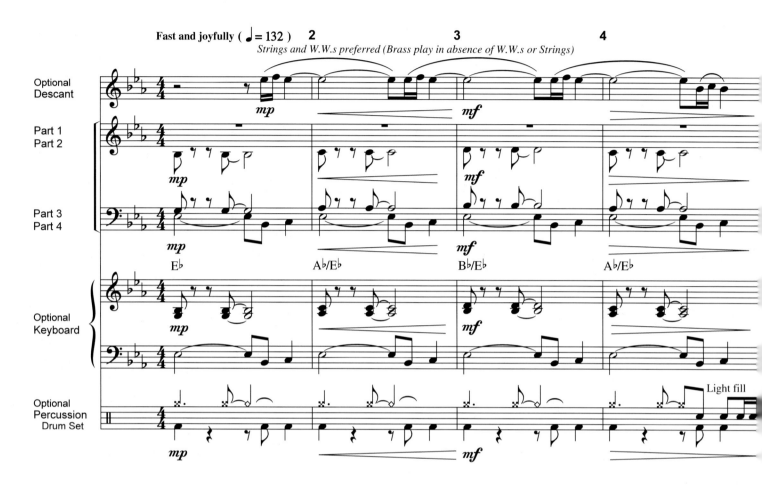

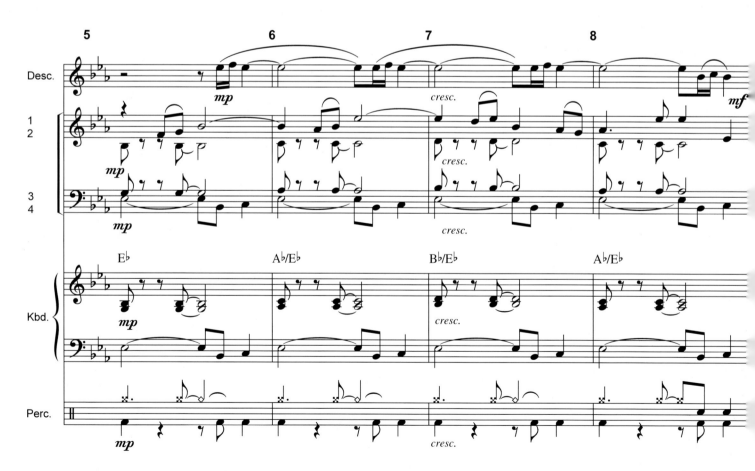

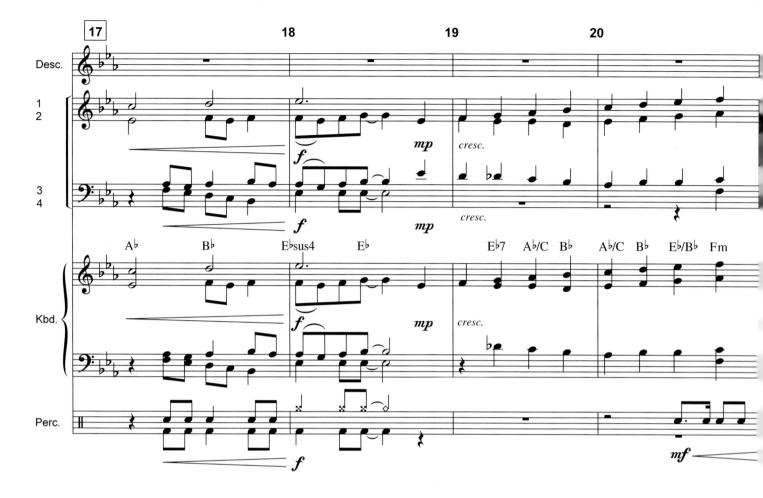

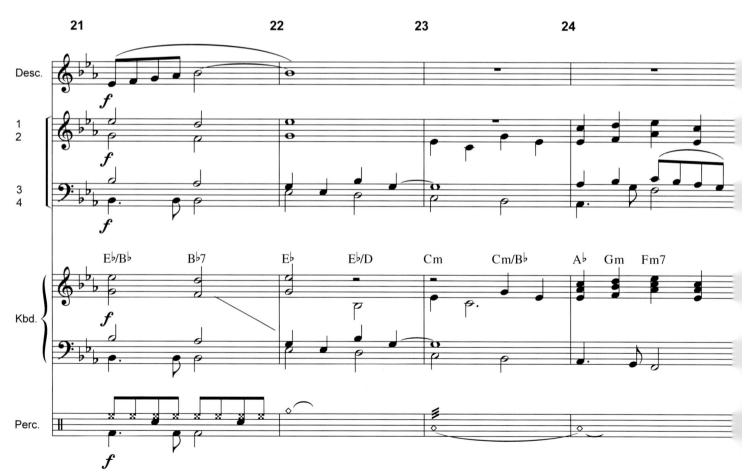

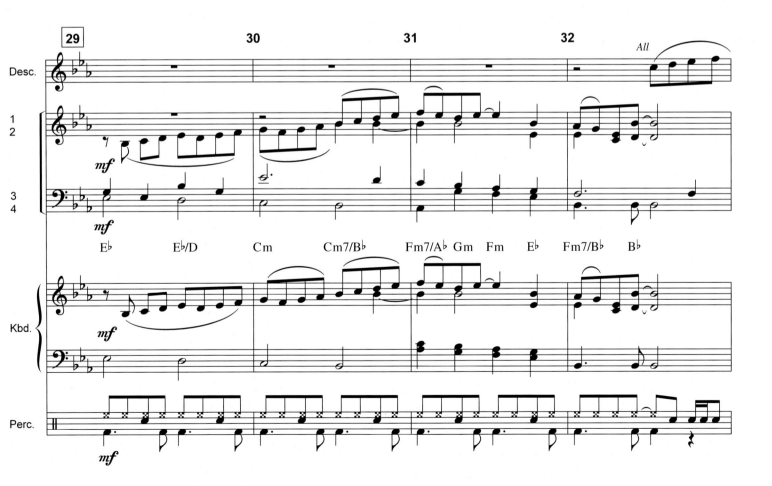

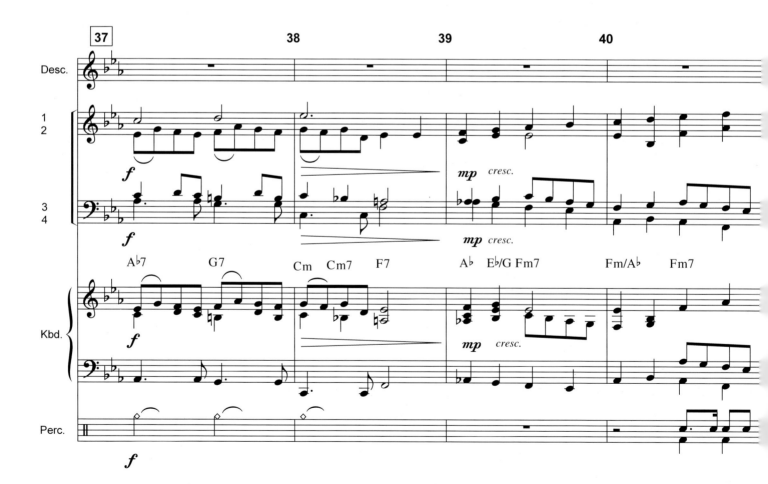

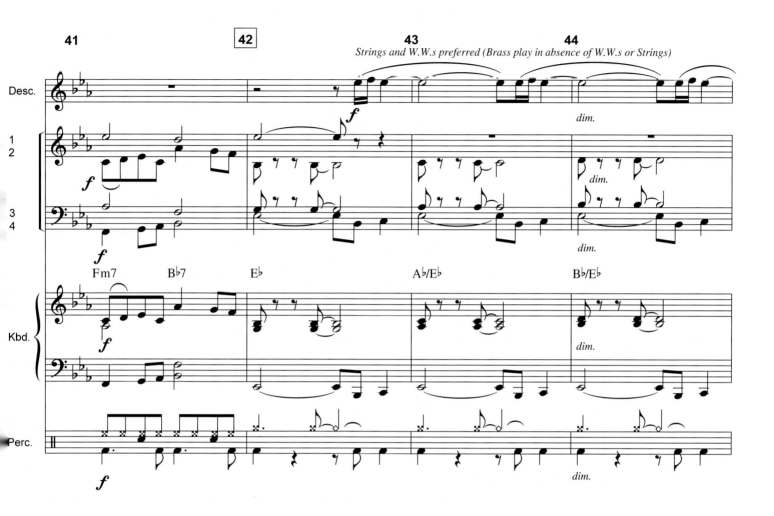

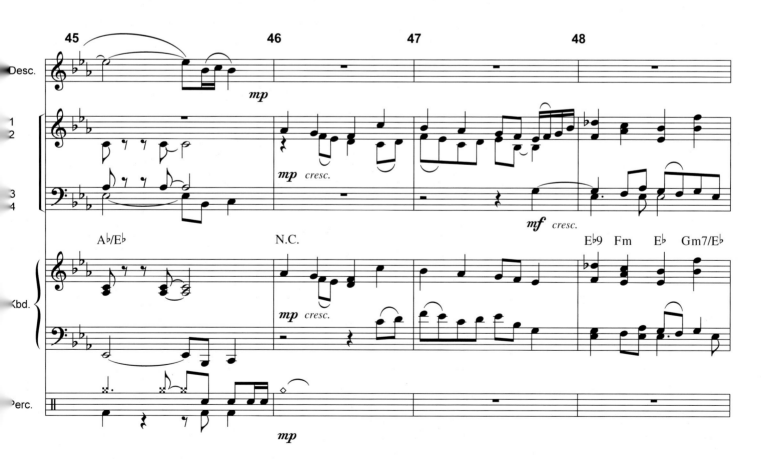

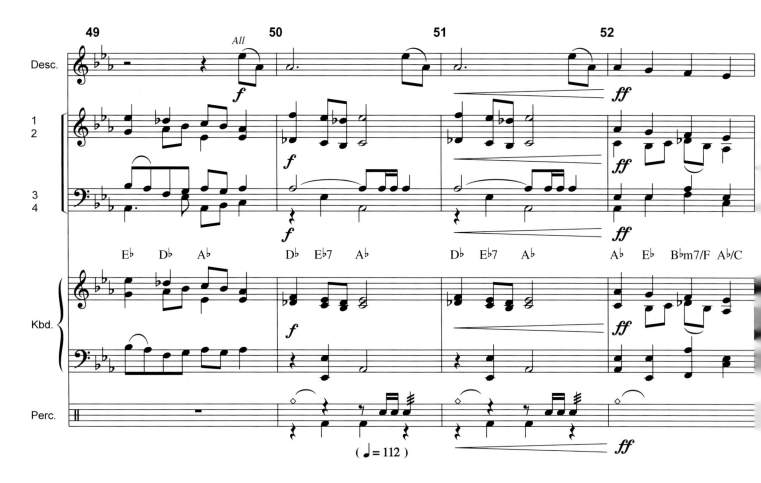

GLORY HALLELUJAH

Patriotic Medley

Timothy Johnson (ASCAP)

Brass preferred (W.W.s or Strings play
in absence of Brass)

CHRIST THE LORD IS RISEN TODAY

Stephen Bulla (ASCAP)

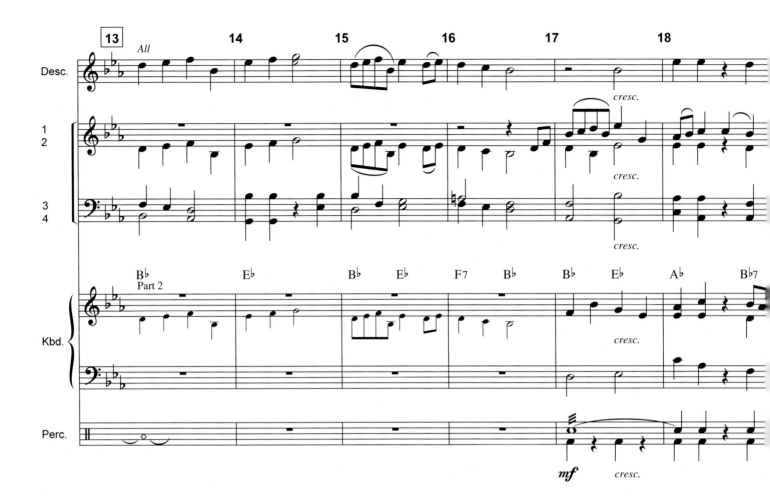

COME, YE THANKFUL PEOPLE, COME

Douglas Court (ASCAP)

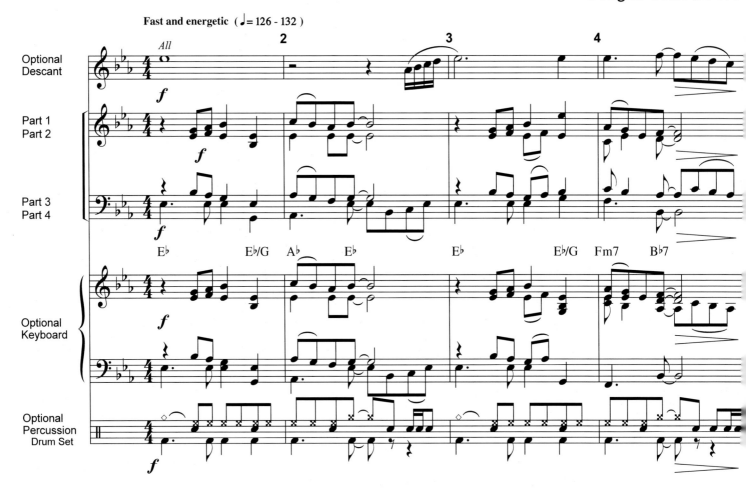

Strings and W.W.s preferred
(Brass play in absence of W.W.s or Strings)

CHRISTMAS BELLS

Carol of the Bells / Come, All Ye Shepherds

James Curnow (ASCAP)

Strings and W.W.s preferred (Brass play in absence of W.W.s or Strings)

62

POLISH CAROL

James Curnow (ASCAP)

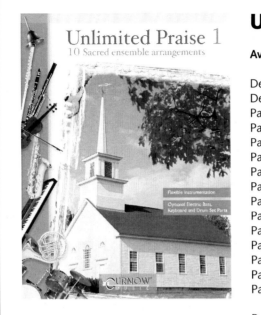

UNLIMITED PRAISE 1

Available for:

Descant C	Flute, Oboe, Bells, Violin	CMP 0551-01
Descant B♭	B♭ Clarinet, B♭ Trumpet	CMP 0551-01
Part 1 C	Flute, Oboe, Bells, Violin	CMP 0552-01
Part 1 B♭	B♭ Clarinet, B♭ Trumpet	CMP 0553-01
Part 1 E♭	E♭ Alto Saxophone, E♭ Trumpet, E♭ Clarinet	CMP 0554-01
Part 2 C	Violin	CMP 0555-01
Part 2 B♭	B♭ Clarinet, B♭ Trumpet 1	CMP 0556-01
Part 2 F	F Horn, English Horn	CMP 0557-01
Part 2 E♭	E♭ Alto Saxophone, E♭ Alto Horn	CMP 0558-01
Part 3 B.C.	Bassoon, Trombone, Euphonium, Cello	CMP 0559-01
Part 3 C	Viola	CMP 0560-01
Part 3 B♭	B♭ Tenor Saxophone, B♭ Euphonium T.C.	CMP 0561-01
Part 3 F	F Horn	CMP 0562-01
Part 3 E♭	E♭ Alto Clarinet, E♭ Alto Saxophone, E♭ Alto Horn	CMP 0563-01
Part 4 B.C.	Bassoon, Trombone, Euphonium, Tuba, Cello, Double Bass	CMP 0564-01
Part 4 B♭ T.C.	B♭ Bass Clarinet, B♭ Contra Bass Clarinet, B♭ Euphonium T.C., B♭ Bass T.C.	CMP 0565-01
Part 4 E♭ T.C.	E♭ Contralto Clarinet, E♭ Baritone Saxophone, E♭ Bass T.C.	CMP 0566-01
Keyboard	Piano, Synthesizer, Organ (Guitar Chords included)	CMP 0567-01
Percussion	Drum Set	CMP 0568-01
Electric Bass	Electric Bass, Double Bass	CMP 0569-01
Score		CMP 0517-01

THE YOUNG BAND CHRISTMAS COLLECTION

Available for:

Flute	CMP 0941-05
Oboe	CMP 0942-05
B♭ Clarinet 1	CMP 0943-05
B♭ Clarinet 2	CMP 0944-05
B♭ Bass Clarinet	CMP 0945-05
E♭ Alto Saxophone	CMP 0946-05
B♭ Tenor Saxophone	CMP 0947-05
E♭ Baritone Saxophone	CMP 0948-05
B♭ Trumpet 1	CMP 0949-05
B♭ Trumpet 2	CMP 0950-05
F Horn	CMP 0951-05
Trombone/Euphonium B.C./Bassoon	CMP 0952-05
B♭ Euphonium T.C.	CMP 0953-05
Tuba	CMP 0954-05
Mallet Percussion	CMP 0976-05
Timpani	CMP 0955-05
Percussion 1	CMP 0956-05
Percussion 2	CMP 0977-05
E♭ Horn	CMP 0957-05
B♭ Trombone/B♭ Euphonium/B♭ Bass T.C.	CMP 0953-05
B♭ Trombone/B♭ Euphonium/B♭ Bass B.C./E♭ Bass B.C.	CMP 0958-05
E♭ Bass T.C.	CMP 0948-05

CURNOW
MUSIC